Managing Court Cases with Mental Strength

Siva Prasad Bose

pencil

ISBN 978-93-5610-123-4

Published in India 2022 by Pencil

Contributors:
Co-Author: Joy Bose

A brand of
One Point Six Technologies Pvt. Ltd.
123, Building J2, Shram Seva Premises,
Wadala Truck Terminal, Wadala (E)
Mumbai 400037, Maharashtra, INDIA
E connect@thepencilapp.com
W www.thepencilapp.com

Author biography

Siva Prasad Bose is a writer of introductory guidebooks related to Indian laws. He is currently retired after many years of service in Uttar Pradesh Power Corporation Limited. He received his engineering degree from Jadavpur University, Kolkata and has a law degree from Meerut University, Meerut. His interests lie in the fields of family law, civil law, law of contracts, and areas of law related to power electricity related issues.

CONTENTS

Preface

Sometimes we cannot avoid court cases. In India sometimes they can run for many months or years. We may have to attend the hearings in different cities. Combined with this are problems with handling a lawyer, cross examinations, unexpected surprises from the opposite party and other issues.

Court cases can thus take a huge toll not only on our finances but also our physical and mental health. Sometimes we may feel helpless and fall into deep stress or depression.

However, all court cases do not have to end up this way. We can train to manage them in a more meaningful and productive way. We need to treat court cases as just part of our lives and not everything, just like the other parts of our lives. In short, we need to train how to handle court cases properly with as less stress as possible. This requires special techniques to cultivate our mental strength.

In this book, we study some of the techniques on how to handle court cases and balance our lives while dealing with them. We do not focus on the different types of court cases and legal remedies, but rather focus on the psychology of managing court cases and how to make the process less stressful. Our main focus remains civil cases between litigating parties, however some of the advice and strategies can be applied for ongoing criminal cases as well. Also, we write this book from the point of view of the litigants, rather than the lawyers or other players of the justice system.

Acknowledgements

In preparing this book, the authors would like to acknowledge advice from different sources including Dr. Arvind Raj from NIMHANS, Vijay VJ from the well-being volunteers, the men's community center in Bangalore, and countless other discussions with various people.

Problems due to court cases

Court cases can lead to all kinds of problems for us. This can include not only financial problems, but also physical and mental problems related to increased stress due to the ongoing cases. In a place like India, where court cases sometimes run for years or even decades, this problem assumes even bigger proportions.

In this chapter, we list some of the types of mental problems we can have while fighting a court case. These are separate from the legal aspects of the court cases, but equally important. It is said that unless we cannot identify the problems accurately, we cannot deal with them properly. That is why we aim to first identify the different kinds of problems that can arise, aside from the direct issues related with the case being fought.

1.1 Psychology of fighting a court case

Court cases are generally brought when the litigants cannot see an easier way to resolve a particular issue. This is mainly applicable for civil court cases. In criminal court cases, the litigant might have committed an offence and is liable for justice as per the law of the land.

Therefore, by its nature, a court case is a desperate measure which is taken when alternative courses of action such as negotiation are exhausted, or the litigants have lost hope of alternative actions achieving the desired results.

The litigants may be coming with a sense of desperation combined with a sense of over-reliance and undue trust in the justice system, and hope that it would deliver them victory. This trust may be contrary to the data that suggests that court cases, especially in India can drag on for years, and there can exist widespread corruption in the Indian court system and institutions which includes police, lawyers, judges etc. Hence, even though the litigant may morally feel they are in the right, it may not translate to results in the actual court judgment.

Sometimes this trust can be due to inexperience and ignorance of the actual court procedures and systems, and not realizing that the case may drag on for years and cost a lot of money and stress, and even after that it may not lead to the desired outcomes which they had when they first started the court case.

On top of the original problem that caused the court case, there is the added sadness that comes from fighting with litigants, who may be family members or close acquaintances. Added to that is the pain of getting a suitable lawyer, of attending each court date, of making the case files and petitions, of deciphering the judgments, and so on. If adverse intermediate or final judgments are passed, then it is an added problem. If the judge turns out to be corrupt or biased, that is an added problem. If the judge gets changed in the middle of the case, or if one has to change the lawyer, that is an added problem. If the lawyer turns out to be less than ideal, that is an added problem. If one has to cross examine the opposite party or themselves undergo a cross examination, then it is an added problem. If the opposite party are threatening you or acting against you while the court case is going on, then it is an added problem.

To conclude, a court case is a painful but unavoidable process and needs careful planning and managing in order to make it more bearable.

1.2 Systemic problems with the court system

In India, the cases typically move at a snail's pace and the whole court system has a huge backlog of millions of cases, combined with lack of judges. Hence, the judges have no time or incentive to read all the case files and pay adequate attention to any case. This leads to cases getting short hearings of only a few minutes on each date and next dates being announced again and again for years on end.

Figure 1. The stress of court case hearings can be overwhelming at times

1.3 Financial Problems

Given that civil court cases in India can drag on for years, the financial burden can be considerable. The cost of hiring a competent lawyer in big cities can run into lakhs and sometimes crores, and increase with the number of years and the number of court cases for the same client which that lawyer is fighting.

1.4 Problems related to lawyers

Often, our lawyer may turn out to be less than ideal. This may be in the following ways:

- Our lawyer might be not experienced in the specific area of law that the court case deals with.
- They might be too much busy with multiple cases from multiple clients to fight our case properly.
- They may lose interest in the case as time drags on.
- They might treat us (the client) as a cash cow and encourage us to file more cases that do not bring any concrete results but just increase the time and costs and additional stress.

- They might not be familiar with new technology and how to e-file a case or use emails.

- They might be overconfident and overbearing and not listen to the client's needs, insisting that they know what is best, and thus harm the client's position.

- They might simply refuse to act as per the instructions from the client, selecting the course of action that lead to least effort for themselves.

- Worst of all, they may collude with the opposite party and compromise the case at crucial points.

1.5 Problems related to unfamiliar procedures

The unfamiliarity of the court environment can give to added stress for the litigants. There may be specific procedures on where and how to file various documents, how to draft and send legal notices, and so on. A client may not be aware of these procedures. They might be completely dependent on their lawyer or advocate for all these tasks, and the lawyer may not deal with them with sufficient seriousness and timeliness. The judges might get changed in the middle of the case and court cases might get postponed or delayed due to unforeseen events like accidents, strikes or pandemics like Covid. All this could be further complicated if the person is living in a different city than where the case is running.

1.6 Problems related to unfamiliar laws

A litigant might be unfamiliar with the exact civil or criminal laws applicable to their case, or previous judgments in similar cases. This could give rise to feelings of uncertainty, leading to more stress. Different stages of the case, different kinds of arguments and evidence by the opposite party could call for different kinds of laws and judgments to be applied. Again, they would have to completely depend on their lawyer to decide which laws to argue for or against.

1.7 Problems related to adverse judgments and surprises by the opposite party

The opposite party in the case can bring all kinds of unexpected last-minute surprises, such as new unseen evidence, new arguments or new strategies. Sometimes the judge may pronounce adverse judgments. Combined with other factors such as inability to understand the court process and the lawyer not making the right arguments, this could lead to feelings of helplessness and lack of control, which could be a source of additional stress for the litigants.

1.8 Problems related to travel for the court case

Sometimes, the court case may be running in a different city and the litigants would need to rearrange their schedules and take leave from work and travel to the city on different court dates. This can be an additional cause of stress.

1.9 Problems related to stress and mental health

In any ongoing litigation, stress can be a major problem for the litigants. This can manifest in different ways such as increased irritability, decreased productivity, a reduced quality of life, withdrawal from society and so on. This can also affect the family members of the litigants who are in close contact with them. The mental health can also be affected leading to different kinds of symptoms such as depression.

1.10 Problems related to physical health

Ongoing court cases, and their accompanying stress, can take a heavy toll on the physical health of the litigants. All kinds of diseases can crop up due to a reduced immune response due to stress. Existing diseases such as diabetes can become worse as well. Lack of sleep, lack of exercise can be additional symptoms of poor physical health due to the stress of ongoing litigation.

1.11 Problems related to family, jobs and other commitments

Court cases are just one part of life. The litigants would have other responsibilities such as delivering in their daily jobs, paying their bills and housing loan EMIs, taking care of their family including spouse, kids, elderly parents and other dependents and so on. Meeting all these existing commitments as well as dealing with the stress of the court cases can be too much for some people to handle.

1.12 Conclusion

In this chapter we have discussed a few kinds of problems that can increase our stress due to ongoing court cases. In the following chapters, we will discuss ways and means to deal with these problems.

General strategies to deal with court cases

In this chapter, we look at a few general strategies to deal with the various problems related to ongoing court cases. These strategies can be useful no matter what is the type of the case or what is the exact nature of the problems a litigant may be facing. In subsequent chapters, we will return to discussing specific problems and their strategies.

2.1 Having a long-term view

Instead of having a short-term aim of winning this court case, one should keep a long-term view and keep things in perspective. This includes the following:

- We should always remember that our court cases are a small part of life and not the only part.
- We should keep in mind that losing or winning cases may not be completely in our hands, and we have to accept what happens rather than have undue expectations that everything will go in our favor, even if we strongly feel we are in the right.
- Even if we get some judgments that are not in our favor, we should not allow such short term

setbacks to affect our quality of life and always keep the bigger picture in mind.

- Similarly, if we get some judgments that do go in our favor, we should not be overwhelmed unduly and rather look at the bigger picture.

2.2 Getting a clear idea of our priorities

During the running of the court case, it is a good idea to reflect and keep reminding ourselves of our real priorities and aims in life. This includes the following reflections to think about regularly:

- Reflect on what do we really want from life? What were we born for, what is our mission in life, what will we regret if we are on our death bed?

- Reflect on whether the court case will really give us what we want, or is it just a small part of our life that we have to deal with like everything else we may or may not like, such as the traffic?

- Reflect on our values: Do we really value what we have been gifted with? Do we truly value our family and friends? Do we truly value our job and workmates and the place we live in and the people who work for us?

- We should make it a practice to remind ourselves daily and multiple times what we are grateful for.

- We should think of our happy moments in life, of how we have benefited from the kindness of so many people in small and large ways. We should also think of the people who are less fortunate than we are and resolve to help them all we can.

All this will help us to keep things in perspective and not be overwhelmed with the difficulties of the case or be disheartened when some judgments might go against us.

2.3 Staying physically healthy

It is important to remember to stay physically healthy while fighting our court cases. This includes remembering the following:

- Have a proper breakfast and 3 meals daily at regular times

- Have proper 6-8 hours sleep at the same time daily

- Do some exercise such as gym or yoga or simply walk or jog at least 5000 steps daily.

- Have regular medical checkups and take our medicines regularly if prescribed by the doctor.

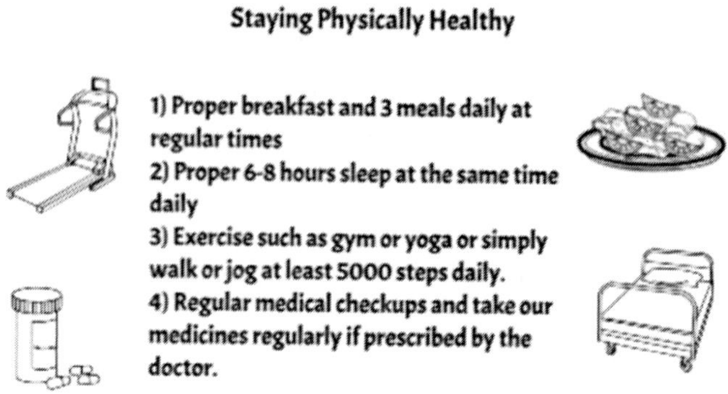

Figure 2. Regular steps to take in order to stay physically healthy

2.4 Balancing our commitments

We may have multiple commitments in our life, which can include work commitments, commitments to our family and to the wider society. When we are feeling trapped in an ongoing court case, it is very easy to lose sight of our existing commitments. Not fulfilling some of our commitments might may end up further increasing our stress and in our feeling like a failure. At the same time, we should be aware that we have only a limited store of energy and we have to prioritize what we can best do with the time and resources that are available to us.

Figure 3. An illustration of balancing our various commitments

One way to make sure that we are keeping our commitments is to become more organized, keep an updated calendar, make our work areas separated and clean and un-cluttered. We should periodically do an audit of exactly where our time is being spent each day. We should aim to balance our time commitments of the following:

- Work time, spent in our office work
- Family time, spent with our immediate family
- Me-time, reserved for our inner reflections
- Social time with friends

We should aim to balance our time commitments on a weekly or monthly basis, if balancing them daily is difficult.

Similar to time commitments, we should also aim to meet our financial and other commitments.

2.5 Dealing with feelings of helplessness and loss of control

In the early days of the case, we might have been filled with hope that we will quickly win the case and our objectives will be met. As the case drags on, this hope may slowly die and we may realize that we are trapped in a case that can drag for years, cost a lot of money and may not even produce the result we want. This may lead to our getting a feeling of helplessness and loss of control.

Some ways to combat such thoughts and feelings of helplessness are as follows:

- We should cultivate an attitude of acceptance. We should humbly accept whatever judgment s and situations we find ourselves in.

- We should not try to control what we cannot control, since all the factors related to our case are not in our hands.

- We should remind ourselves that life has its ups and downs and it is futile to try to control everything.

- We should remember that it is our duty to fight to the best of our ability, but we should not become unduly attached to getting a positive result, as

Lord Krishna had advised Arjuna in the Bhagavad Gita.

- We should also keep reminding ourselves of the bigger picture and what is most important in our lives, more important than the ongoing court cases.

Using the above reflections, we may be able to deal with negative thoughts and feelings of helplessness with respect to the cases.

2.6 Conclusion

In this chapter we have looked at some general strategies in brief, which we can use in handling different kinds of court cases. In the following chapters, we will go deeper into some specific strategies for different aspects of the cases.

Dealing with case related issues

In the previous chapter, we discussed some general strategies that can be useful while handling our cases. In this chapter, we look at some specific issues related to fighting court cases.

3.1. Applying Sun Tzu's Art of War to fighting our court cases

Sun Tzu's book "The Art of War" is a text of conflict in all domains including actual wars, politics, and even corporate boardrooms. It was written by Sun Tzu, a very successful and brilliant Chinese general and military strategist of the 5th century BC, based on his experience of fighting many wars in early China and managing rebellions within the kingdom. By studying and applying lessons from this book, we can develop strategies on how to deal with our ongoing court cases as well.

Some of the ways in which we can apply the teachings from the book to our court cases are as follows:

The foremost advice in the art of war is to know oneself and know the enemy, and then act accordingly. In order to do so, we have to dispassionately and logically make a list of exactly where our strengths and weaknesses lie, so as to leverage the same in the best possible way. In the same way, we should evaluate our opponents in the court case as well.

Figure 4. The book "The Art of War" by Sun Tzu

The art of war says that the best war is one that is not needed to be fought. War is destructive in nature, however at the core it is just a mechanism to resolve a dispute or grievance. If the same dispute can be resolved by other, less destructive, means, then war is unnecessary. Having said that, a good general needs to be prepared for all eventualities including how to fight a war if it comes to that. Knowing this, we should try and explore other tactics and strategies, such as ongoing negotiations through third parties, to resolve the issue, in parallel with the court cases.

The text also says that all warfare is based on deception. It is better to make the enemy think we are strong when we are actually weak, or vice versa. We must keep them guessing of our actual strategy, while making every effort to know and preempt their strategy. Therefore, at each step in the cases, we should reflect on the respective positions of ourselves and the opposite party. Based on that, we should re-evaluate ours and theirs strengths and weaknesses. Based on that, we should decide our next legal strategies, or what to ask our lawyer and judge to focus on.

We should also keep in mind the bigger picture, what is the ultimate objective? Is it just winning the case or getting peace of mind. There is no point of winning a small court case and losing the battle of life, which includes one's career, health, well-being and other relationships.

Keeping these teachings in mind, we should develop a proactive and dynamic strategy to fighting the court cases while being aware of our own and the opponent's strengths and weaknesses, and act accordingly. We should also be prepared to re-evaluate and tweak our strategy as the need may be or as the situation changes.

3.2 Choosing a good lawyer for fighting our court cases

One important strategy for court cases is to get a good and competent lawyer whom we can trust to fight our cases.

We should engage a lawyer who is competent and has prior experience in dealing with such cases in his or her career. We should make sure our lawyer keeps themselves abreast of current knowledge in law including recent judgments, is comfortable with technology such as email and remote hearings. Considering that remote hearings and e-filings have become more common nowadays with the Covid-19 pandemic and are here to stay even after the pandemic is over, we should make sure that our the lawyer too should be comfortable with this.

The most important quality in our chosen lawyer is that they should listen to us and be ready to act as per our instructions. They should not have the attitude that they always know what is best, but rather they should be humble, open minded and respect the fact that the client knows best about his or her own case.

3.3 Managing our lawyer

We should try to skillfully manage the lawyer during the conduct of the case, including negotiating the fees in advance, giving proper incentives and so on. We should also try to be friendly with our lawyer and not pick up fights with them over petty issues. If we decide to change the lawyer, we should try to do so amicably and without fighting.

We can try to use our lawyer in skillful ways, such as sending them to attend the court dates and avoid unnecessary travel.

3.4 Changing our lawyer

We should also not be attached to any one lawyer and be ready to change our lawyer if the need arises, for example if we realize that the current lawyer is no longer able to effectively represent our case.

As per the Indian laws, the existing lawyer cannot stop us from changing our lawyer, even if they do not provide a "No Objection Certificate". We can file a new Wakalatnama in the court certifying that the new lawyer will represent us in this case. We should always keep this in mind.

Having said that, it is also not a good practice to change lawyers too frequently during the case. Having chosen a lawyer, we should not have undue expectations on them and give them some time to prove themselves. We should also try to be amicable while changing the lawyer.

3.5 Dealing with unexpected developments and adverse judgments

One important aspect of a court case is knowing how to deal with unexpected developments including adverse judgments during the court case.

When such adverse judgments happen, we should not become emotional but rather analyze our approach for weaknesses. We should analyze how we are handling the case and whether in hindsight we could have done something differently to not get the adverse judgments. What is done is done, however in future we can try to learn from our past mistakes and not repeat them again.

3.6 Handling our finances

An important part of any court case is handling our finances properly. If not properly planned and budgeted in advance, the costs including the lawyer's fees, cost of hiring new lawyers, cost of filing additional cases, travel related to cases etc. may spiral out of our control and be the cause of additional stress.

Therefore, it is important to first estimate the budget by asking our friends and acquaintances who have dealt with similar cases. We can also research on the internet or on forums such as lawrato.com where one can get advice from lawyers on specific aspects of the law.

Having estimated our budget for the case, we should figure out how to arrange our finances to pay for it. We should also take into account that the case can drag for a longer time and may lead to multiple related cases rather than just a single case. Even if we cannot estimate a fixed number given all kinds of varying costs, we should budget for a certain approximate sum every year the case runs,

In times when we have to make finance related decisions, such as if our lawyer advises us to file an additional case or go for a strategy that costs us money, we should do a proper cost benefit analysis before deciding to allocate extra funds.

The same goes for how to pay the lawyer's fees. We should negotiate paying them in installments rather than the entire fee at once, and also make it dependent on how long the case runs.

3.7 The art of cross examination

Sometimes, we may be cross examined by the opposite party, during the conduct of the case. Or else, we may have to advise our own lawyer on how to cross examine the opposite party and what questions to ask them. It is important to prepare properly for such an eventuality. We should act as our own devil's advocate and prepare a list of questions as well as the opposite party's probable answers to all such questions. We should even practice the cross-examination session with a friend or simply in front of a mirror. We should not take it lightly but try our best to give the prepared answers as per our strategy so as not to weaken our case. Similarly, we should prepare the questions for the opposite party based on a close analysis of their position and how best to weaken their case. We should go over the questions carefully with our lawyer beforehand.

3.8 Conclusion

In this chapter we have looked at specific strategies that can be practically used to deal with court case related issues.

Dealing with stress

As mentioned earlier, ongoing court cases can cause us a great deal of stress. In this chapter, we discuss the ways in which this stress can affect us and ways in which we can deal with it.

4.1 The Stress Cycle

Stress normally works in a cycle. The cycle works as follows:

- We may get stressed because of a variety of factors including ongoing court cases.
- Because of stress, we can manifest different kinds of reactions. We may turn to overeating or alcohol to deal with the stress. Stress may lead to bodily symptoms such as increased heart rate, short breaths, high blood pressure, diabetes, indigestion and so on. We can become more prone to negative emotions such as anger. Our behavior may become moody and unpredictable and fluctuating. Our ability to function socially might become worse and we may become withdrawn from our friends and relatives. We may indulge in

negative self-talk such as thinking that we are worthless or failures. We may become less able to concentrate and more prone to get distracted.

- All these could lead to worse effects such as heart diseases, mental illnesses, affect our memory and sleep, cause premature aging and so on.

- This could lead to lesser enjoyment and productivity in life, leading to even greater stress.

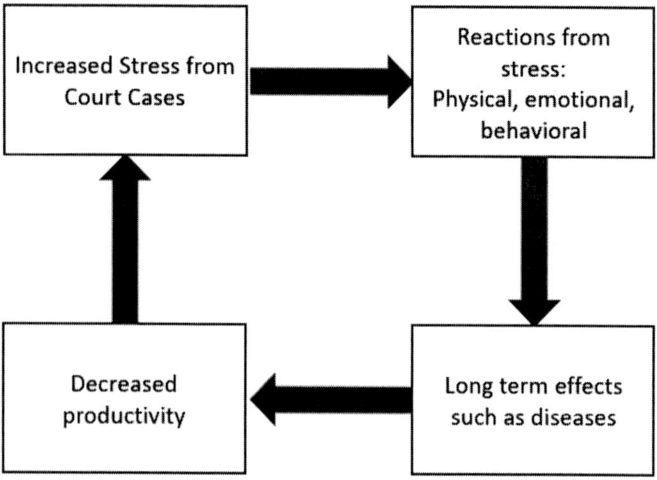

Figure 5. Illustration of the stress cycle

This stress cycle goes on and on, increasing our stress and further decreasing our ability to deal with our ongoing court cases.

4.2 Systematic ways to tackle stress

In order to tackle stress and break the stress cycle, we can follow a few simple steps, which are as follows:

- We should aim to have regular meals and good sleep.
- We should aim to keep active including a regular exercise schedule. For example, we can do a few simple yoga exercises, such as a few cycles of "surya namaskara" yoga exercise.
- We should cultivate some hobbies to keep our brain active.
- We should make it a point to keep meeting our close friends and well-wishers.
- We should not indulge in negative thoughts including blaming others for our problems, or try to control everything including the way our court cases are going.
- We should try and balance our time, keeping adequate me-time for ourselves as well as allocate enough time for our family.

By following all the above steps, we would be able to improve our mental health and be stronger and better able to deal with the court cases.

4.3 Simple techniques to combat stress

We can check ourselves from time to time if we are having the symptoms of stress such as short breath. If so, we can follow a few simple techniques to come out of stress.

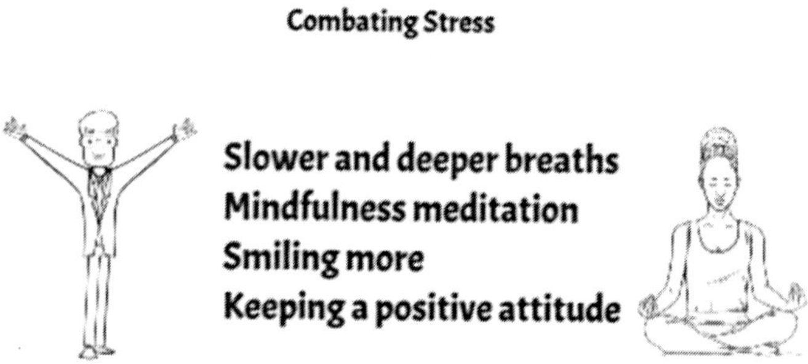

Figure 6. Steps for combating stress

4.3.1 Longer and slower breaths

One technique can be to consciously make our breath longer and deeper, make sure our breath is slower and reaches all the way till the stomach. This technique has the immediate effect of lowering our stress level.

4.3.2 Mindfulness meditation

Another technique for lowering stress can be to follow mindfulness meditation for a few minutes daily. This involves sitting with our back straight, closing our eyes, mindfully observing the various sensations of our body slowly from head to toe, and counting the breath from 1 to 10 and again restarting at 1.

4.3.3 Smiling more

One way to beat stress can be simply to smile more. The act of smiling tricks our brain into thinking we are happy and relaxed, and the body also exhibits the symptoms of relaxation rather than stress.

4.3.4 Reframing and keeping a positive attitude

Another way to combat stress is to keep a positive attitude. This can be done in the following ways:

- Every morning we can bring to mind all the things we are grateful for, all the people who have helped us and are helping us in our life.

- We can make positive affirmations such as "may myself and others be happy and well", and "may all the people around us also be happy and well".

- We can try to mentally forgive our opponents in the case, as well as any others we may be having grudges against.

- We can encourage ourselves with positive self-talk encouraging ourselves, as opposed to negative self-talk.

- We can think of the court cases almost as a test of our patience and a training for us to become mentally stronger.

- We can use this opportunity to think of other people who are caught in court cases like us, empathize with them and wish them well and hope they can get out of their cases successfully.

- We can take the opportunity to help people around us in ways big and small, which has the side effect of improving our own mental health and relieving our own stress.

By following the above steps regularly and sustained over a period of time, we might be able to combat stress effectively and start a "wellness cycle" that can fight the stress cycle.

4.4 Cultivating a carefree attitude in life

One way to reduce our stress in court cases and more generally is to cultivate a carefree attitude to whatever happens in our life. We should not always try to control everything or expect things to go well. The whole of our life is a learning process and we should be aware of this.

In order to cultivate this attitude, we should not be unduly concerned with what is happening or what others may be thinking of us. We should make it a habit to take free time off or ourselves and take regular breaks from work and other commitments such as court cases, and take regular walks and retreats in the midst of nature.

We should also endeavor to cultivate a child like inquisitive mind no matter what our age, since it helps our brain to continue making new connections, become more efficient and think of different out of the box and creative ways to deal with our cases.

4.5 Conclusion

In this chapter, we have looked at some practical ways and means to get relief from stress, at least in the short term. This can be applied for dealing with the court cases, both when we are feeling stressed inside the court or when worrying about the cases when at home.

Using Cognitive model and Cognitive Behavioral Therapy

In the earlier chapters we have suggested a few mechanisms by which to handle the court cases and reduce stress and related symptoms. In this chapter we look at the cognitive model of psychotherapy and explore how it can be used to better handle our court cases.

5.1 The cognitive model

An American psychologist named Aaron Beck introduced the cognitive model of psychology in 1960s. as per this model, our thoughts affect our behavior and feelings. Hence, to deal with court cases related stress, one key way is to examine our thoughts and beliefs and assumptions and understand how they are affecting our feelings and behavior.

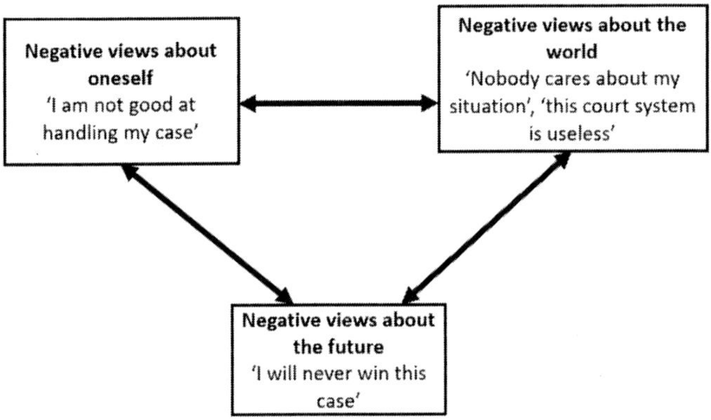

Figure 7. Illustration about the cognitive triad, how negative thoughts about oneself, the world and future feed into each other

One of the ways this works is via the cognitive triad as shown in figure 4. This comprises the following:

- Negative views about oneself, such as "I am worthless at handling my case"
- Negative views about the world, such as "the court system is useless and cannot help me"
- Negative views about the future, such as "I am never going to win my court case"

These negative views feed into each other and create a spiral of ever more negative thinking. This can adversely affect our health and well-being.

The way out is to understand how this negative cycle of thoughts really works, and then try to combat the same using positive thoughts and questioning our negative assumptions that are not grounded in reality.

For example, the negative thought "I am worthless at handling my case" can be combatted by carefully bringing to mind our past success in fighting the case: we have successfully been fighting the case till this long, we have gathered the evidence, fixed the lawyer and paid their fees etc.

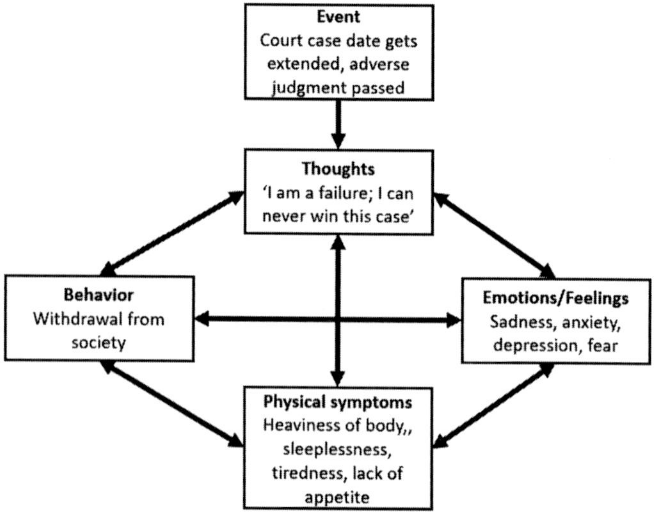

Figure 8. Illustration about how negative events in court cases can affect our feelings, thoughts, physical symptoms and behavior, as per the cognitive model in psychology

5.2 Understanding the link between behavior, thinking and emotions

As per the cognitive model in psychology, there is a link between our thinking, emotions, physical sensations and behavior and these feed upon each other.

For example, the following is an example:

External event: Adverse judgement passed in court case, court case gets deferred.

The above event can produce the following:

Negative thoughts: "I will never win this case", "This case is going on so long without any result", "I am worthless"

Feelings and emotions: sadness, fear, anxiety, depression

Physical sensations: heaviness in the body, lack of sleep, lack of appetite.

This in turn can lead to

Behaviors: such as reduced contact with others, feeling withdrawn, sitting in one place, lying in bed till late in the day and so on.

If this continues for a period of time, conditions such as depression and anxiety, and health issues such as diabetes can result.

This is the way in which negative thoughts related to the court cases can lead to negative feelings and conditions like depression. We should understand the way in which these factors are interlinked, this will help us to form a strategy to break the cycle.

5.3 Using CBT (Cognitive Behavior Therapy) and challenging negative thoughts

Cognitive Behavior Therapy (CBT) was developed by Aaron Beck in 1960s and 1970s and provides a structured framework to break the cycle of negative thoughts. It has been successfully used all over the world in cases of depression, anxiety and other conditions. It follows methods to break the cycle of negative thoughts and cultivate more realistic appraisals of unfavorable situations.

Once we understand the cognitive model as to how negative thoughts about the court cases cause negative feelings and lead to unhelpful behaviors, we can take actions to challenge our negative thoughts and gradually replace them with positive thoughts.

The challenge is to break the negative cycle and link, and for this the method is to question our hidden core beliefs behind our negative thoughts (such as 'I am worthless') using logic and evidence from our past experience.

For this, we should carefully note our momentary thoughts when we have negative emotions and then try to come to the root of those thoughts. Once we have written them down, we should examine how or why such thoughts are coming, and challenge ourselves with the opposite evidence.

An example of this can be as follows: If we receive an unfavorable judgement, we may think that it is our fault and that we are worthless. In actual case, it could be due to reasons beyond our control. In such a case, we should challenge our negative thoughts instead of ruminating on them. We should bring to mind the times when we had successfully handled similar and more challenging situations in life. Therefore, it is incorrect to think that we cannot handle such situations or that we are a failure simply because we got some unfavorable judgment.

5.4 Cultivating positive thoughts

Since we are often prone to focusing unduly on the negative thoughts, one remedy can be to instead deliberately focus on our positive thoughts and experiences.

We can bring to mind our achievements in life, thinking of instances where we have been handling successfully our job and family in the past.

By repeatedly bring to mind and training our mind to focus on the positive aspects and use them to challenge the negative thoughts, we can combat and break the cycle of negativity and thus gain freedom from stress, anxiety and depression leading from our court cases.

5.5 Using Mindfulness along with CBT and positive thoughts

Mindfulness is a way of bringing our notice to the immediate thoughts and feelings at each moment. The most common way to practice mindfulness is to close our eyes and calmly turn our attention to the thoughts, feelings and sensations in the mind and all parts of the body.

One can practice mindfulness in one of these two ways:

- Do a body scan, going systematically from top of the head till the feet, and pay attention to the sensations and feelings from each part systematically.
- Just let the mind free, do not dwell on the thoughts. Bring attention to whichever sensations or feelings are the strongest at that moment.

Mindfulness practice involves cultivating a feeling of acceptance to whatever is happening without thinking too much about it. Using mindfulness with each sensation or thought or feeling, we remain in the present moment without judgment, just mindfully acknowledge the feeling and let it go.

Even when the court cases are not going well and we are suffering from health or financial issues, we can mindfully notice each negative thought as it comes, acknowledge it without dwelling on it and just let it go and return to mindfulness of the body and other sensations.

This practice can be done on a regular basis for a few minutes every day. Once we have gained familiarity with this practice, it can help us to better deal with the negative cycle of thoughts and feelings as we discussed earlier.

5.6 Conclusion

In this chapter we have learnt about the cognitive model that explains how our thoughts are linked to feelings and behaviors. We have also discussed the ways by we can combine the benefits of mindfulness with the CBT techniques of understanding the relation between thoughts and feelings, questioning our negative thoughts and focusing on positive thoughts and experiences. By applying all these to our feelings and thoughts related with the court cases, we can effectively control the stress, anxiety and depression leading from such cases.

Using Behavioral Therapy

In this chapter, we discuss some techniques from behavioral therapy to help with anxiety while handling the court cases.

6.1 Introduction to conditioning and behavioral therapy

Behavioral therapy aims to modify one's behavior using methods such as classical conditioning and operant conditioning to reinforce our desired behavior (not having stress) and decrease the maladaptive behavior (feeling stressed or anxious).

	Positive (adding something)	Negative (taking away something)
Reinforcement (increases behavior)	Positive Reinforcement	Negative Reinforcement
Punishment (decreases behavior)	Positive Punishment	Negative Punishment

Figure 9. Illustration of conditioning, using reinforcement and punishment as a way to train to increase positive behavior and decrease negative ones

Conditioning involves training one to pair a desired stimulus and a response. The technique was first studied by a Russian psychologist named Ivan Pavlov in the 19th century, who paired a bell and a dog's salivation expecting food when the bell was rung.

A common type of conditioning is called operant conditioning. It includes use of punishment and reinforcement as a way to increase or decrease certain behaviors to more desirable ones.

6.2 Application of conditioning to anxiety at court dates

Many times when having court dates, we may feel scared, stressed or anxious dreading what might happen on the next court date. This kind of stress reaction might be automatic, considering that we do not have control over the court system which can feel unfamiliar and unreliable.

One way to control such anxiety is to train ourselves to pair the stressful situation, such as the next court date, with something pleasant, such as a happy memory or music we like. This can be done by consciously recalling the happy memory or playing our favorite music each time we have the feeling of being stressed or anxious at our next court date. This would train our brain to associate the next date with something pleasant instead of unpleasant.

6.3 Training to acclimatize to the court settings using exposure

Another way is to gradually train ourselves to control our fear and stress at the court using gradual exposure. This can be done, for example, by attending some hearings which are not our own. This can help us to become familiar with the atmosphere and to train not to be stressed by exposure to the non-threatening condition (court atmosphere but not our own hearing).

In addition, we can train ourselves to become more relaxed inside the court by consciously breathing more slowly, having a confident body language and smiling more when in the court. Such small actions trick our brain into feeling of relaxed and lowers our stress.

Using logotherapy

In this chapter, we consider logotherapy, a kind of therapy, as a means to finding higher meaning and purpose while fighting the court cases.

7.1 Introduction to logotherapy

The famous psychologist Viktor Frankl in his book "Man's Search for Meaning" proposed a way to deal with situations in life that cause suffering.

His theory was inspired by his own life experience and suffering of being imprisoned in the concentration camps by the Nazis during the holocaust in World War 2. He carefully observed how some inmates of the camps were able to survive the seemingly hopeless situation by thinking of it as a way to a higher meaning. Those who could not visualize a higher meaning or future gave up and could not survive.

Frankl's theory was that as long as we can find some meaning or higher purpose in our suffering, it becomes easier for us to deal with it and bear the suffering.

This theory can be applied to dealing with prolonged court cases.

7.2 Applying logotherapy to find higher meaning

We can use the principles of logotherapy to find higher meaning when fighting court cases.

As per logotherapy, meaning in life can be found in multiple ways, some of which are as follows:

- Self-awareness and self-discovery
- Finding meaning through work
- Finding meaning through hobbies
- Experiencing love: experiences with friends, family and people in social networks
- Developing a positive attitude
- Finding higher meaning in whatever work one is involved: the higher goal in fighting court cases
- Cultivating resilience and fighting spirit when faced with adversity

Although the suffering from the court cases might seem heavy when we are facing it, we should reflect on what can we learn from it and what is the deeper meaning of all this suffering for us. In this sense, it is like a tough teacher for us. But we do gain something from the experience.

We should reflect on how it can teach us to fight and be stronger no matter what life's difficulties are. Someday, the case will be over, and we can look forward to that day. We will then remember how we fought hard for what we believed in, despite all the suffering.

7.3 Conclusion

In this chapter we have considered how logotherapy can be used to find higher meaning and purpose in our court cases. This can help us to cultivate a more positive attitude and combat negative thoughts.

Techniques to cultivate happiness

In this chapter, we discuss a few techniques can be used to cultivate happiness and a positive outlook, that can help us to deal with the ongoing court cases and combat negative thoughts.

8.1 Happiness hormones and stress hormones

In our body, there are some hormones that govern our different emotions and response to different types of situations.

A few of the happiness related hormones are listed as follows:

- Seratonin: This hormone is released in our body when we help others, such as by donating to needy people or even by helping our family and friends. This is one of the happiness hormones.
- Oxytocin: This hormone is triggered on the sensation of touch from our loved ones, such as a hug, and is also associated with happiness.

- Dopamine: This is another of the happiness hormones, and is associated with the feeling of reward or accomplishment, and is released when someone praises us, or we accomplish something.

- Endorphins: These hormones are released when we exercise our body e.g. by running or doing yoga, and also are triggered when we meditate or when we laugh. This is the most common type of happiness hormones.

There are also a few stress related hormones, which are markers of stress in our body. Some of them are as follows:

- Cortisol: This is the main stress hormone. It makes us more alert and ready to face the perceived threat or threats, in the short term. In the long term, when we are subjected to a prolonged period of stress (for example, due to a prolonged court case), this can have an adverse affect on our health.

- Adrenaline: This is the hormone that gives some people a high, and is triggered by the fight or flight response such as a simulated danger in a roller coaster. This too is harmful in the long term.

Knowing about these hormones, the best way to increase our happiness would be to do activities that trigger the happiness hormones as often as we can. For example by having regular exercises or yoga, helping people around us, and doing meditation.

8.2 Happiness by paying attention to simple pleasures in life

Sometimes, simple pleasures in life such as simply having a good time chatting with friends in a cosy environment with good food and drink can bring us happiness. This is the essence of the Danish idea of Hygge, and in some ways also similar to the Swedish idea of fika. We should knowingly try and make time for such simple pleasures.

Figure 10. Illustration of ikigai

8.3 Happiness by discovering our ikigai

Ikigai is a Japanese term meaning life's purpose or calling. The venn diagram about Ikigai in figure 6 gives some idea of what Ikigai means. In short, it is the intersection of what we love to do, what we are good at, what the world needs, and what the world is willing to pay us.

Ideally, we should be able to find purpose and meaning in whatever we do, which includes the ongoing court cases.

However, in the long term we should aim to cultivate a career which matches our ikigai, since that is the way to maximize our happiness with our work.

8.4 Other techniques for happiness

A few other techniques for happiness are listed below:

- Happiness is linked to being in harmony with nature. This can be cultivated by going on walks in the parks or forests (Japanese style 'forest bath' or shinrin-yoku) or a swim in the lake.

- Happiness is also linked with a minimalistic lifestyle. This involves getting rid of stuff we do not really need and simplifying our life, living in a clean environment, being satisfied with what we have instead of craving for more material things.

- Happiness is also linked to having a relaxed attitude to life, to take things easily and slowly, and let go of being too attached to anything, and not let the career or money become a single-minded focus in life.

8.5 Conclusion

In this chapter we have discussed a few strategies for cultivating happiness. By consciously cultivating strategies for happiness, we can focus on the more positive aspects rather than being bogged down by the negativity of the court cases.

Conclusion

In the previous chapters, we have considered various ways to maintain our mental and physical health and balance the various priorities in life while fighting court cases.

The court cases are typically stressful and it is easy to get lost in the dynamics of the case and ignore the toll it is having on our physical and mental health. These are the hidden costs of the case and should be taken into consideration while developing our overall strategy. Also, the court system in India is slow moving, having a huge backlog of cases and too few judges and therefore often fails to deliver justice. All these factors lead to additional stress on the litigants.

Apart from physical and financial health, mental health is extremely important for fighting the cases. It is also the thing that people are most in danger of losing, while the case drags on.

The strategies to manage cases that are described in this book involve prioritizing what is most important, keeping in mind the larger picture and keeping a balance. It involves taking care of ourselves while fighting the cases. We have also discussed a few specific therapy techniques to reduce stress and anxiety in the short term as well as the long term, as well as cultivate positive thinking.

It is hoped that application of some of these techniques would help people who are currently trapped in the court cases, to handle their cases and other responsibilities in a better and more balanced way.